Hidden, Lost, and Discovered
ABANDONED
PLACES

D1301011

Rourke
Educational Media

A Division of
Carson
Dellosa
Education

ESCAPE

Before Reading: *Building Background Knowledge and Vocabulary*

Building background knowledge can help children process new information and build upon what they already know. Before reading a book, it is important to tap into what children already know about the topic. This will help them develop their vocabulary and increase their reading comprehension.

Questions and Activities to Build Background Knowledge:

1. Look at the front cover of the book and read the title. What do you think this book will be about?
2. What do you already know about this topic?
3. Take a book walk and skim the pages. Look at the table of contents, photographs, captions, and bold words. Did these text features give you any information or predictions about what you will read in this book?

Vocabulary: *Vocabulary Is Key to Reading Comprehension*

Use the following directions to prompt a conversation about each word.

- Read the vocabulary words.
- What comes to mind when you see each word?
- What do you think each word means?

Vocabulary Words:
- cataracts
- erupted
- mining
- nuclear
- radiation
- residents

During Reading: *Reading for Meaning and Understanding*

To achieve deep comprehension of a book, children are encouraged to use close reading strategies. During reading, it is important to have children stop and make connections. These connections result in deeper analysis and understanding of a book.

Close Reading a Text

During reading, have children stop and talk about the following:

- Any confusing parts
- Any unknown words
- Text to text, text to self, text to world connections
- The main idea in each chapter or heading

Encourage children to use context clues to determine the meaning of any unknown words. These strategies will help children learn to analyze the text more thoroughly as they read.

When you are finished reading this book, turn to the next-to-last page for After-Reading Questions and an Activity.

Table of Contents

Bodie, California

NORTH
AMERICA

ATLANTIC
OCEAN

PACIFIC
OCEAN

Tikal, Guatemala

SOUTH
AMERICA

ATLANTIC
OCEAN

SOU

Some cities have no **residents**. The homes, markets, and schools are empty. Without any people, what would you find in these abandoned places?

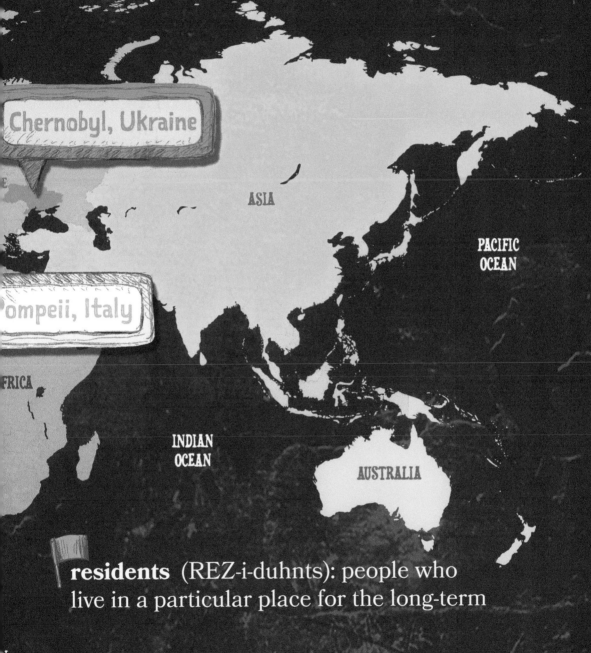

Chernobyl, Ukraine

Pompeii, Italy

ASIA

PACIFIC OCEAN

AFRICA

INDIAN OCEAN

AUSTRALIA

residents (REZ-i-duhnts): people who live in a particular place for the long-term

ANTARCTICA

Chernobyl, Ukraine

A **nuclear** power plant in Chernobyl, Ukraine performed a safety test in April 1986. During the test there was a sudden power surge. The workers tried to press the emergency shutdown button, but it didn't work. Instead, they heard two explosions.

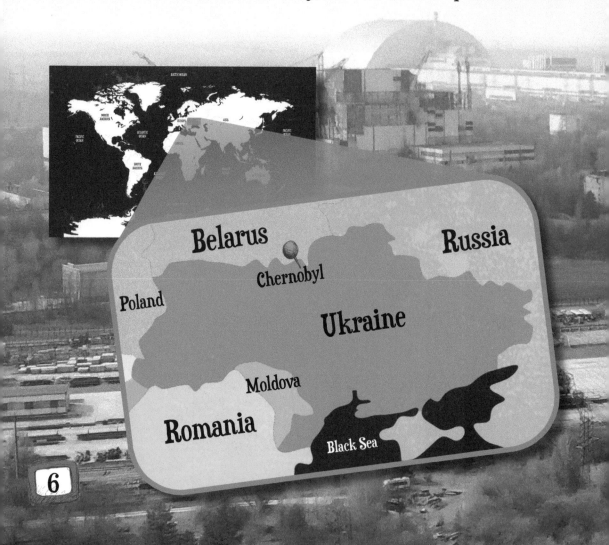

nuclear (NOO-klee-ur): having to do with the energy created by splitting atoms

The explosions sent dangerous **radiation** into the air. People had to evacuate the city. They were told it would only be temporary. But that wasn't true. Now scientists think it will be 20,000 years until it is safe to live there again.

radiation (ray-dee-AY-shuhn): atomic particles that are sent out from a radioactive substance

Chernobyl, Ukraine

Today, wildlife is returning to Chernobyl. But scientists have found negative effects of radiation on the wildlife. Many birds and mammals have **cataracts** in their eyes. The good bacteria and insects that wildlife needs aren't there.

Risky Tourists

Tourists can visit Chernobyl, but there are dangers. Experts suggest that visitors wear clothes they can throw away, masks, gloves, and that they stay away from plants.

cataracts (KAT-uh-raktz): cloudy areas on the lens of the eyes that can cause blindness or partial blindness

Bodie, California

In 1852 gold was discovered near Mono Lake in California, United States. The town of Bodie was built around it. Soon 10,000 people were living there, hoping to get rich from gold **mining**.

mining (mine-ing): digging up minerals that are in the ground

Thirty-four years later most of the gold was gone. Many of the residents moved away in search of other work. By 1942, Bodie was a ghost town.

Bodie, California

Bodie became a State Historic Park in 1962. The town looks like it did when it was abandoned. Stores still have cans on their shelves. There are beds, chairs, and dishes in the houses. People can tour Bodie to see what life was like in the old mining town.

Illegal Souvenirs

Stealing is a problem in Bodie. Tourists come and take little things they find, like a cup or a shoe. A park ranger had the idea to start the rumor that anything taken from Bodie is cursed. People started mailing back the stolen objects with apology letters.

Tikal, Guatemala

Tikal, or Yax Mutal in Mayan, was a Maya city. Historians believe people first lived there around 900 B.C.E. The written records found at Tikal show it was a very important place, like a capital city for the Maya.

Tikal, Guatemala

Tikal was eventually abandoned. Historians don't know exactly why the Maya left Tikal. It is believed that war, overpopulation, deforestation, and lack of food led to their leaving.

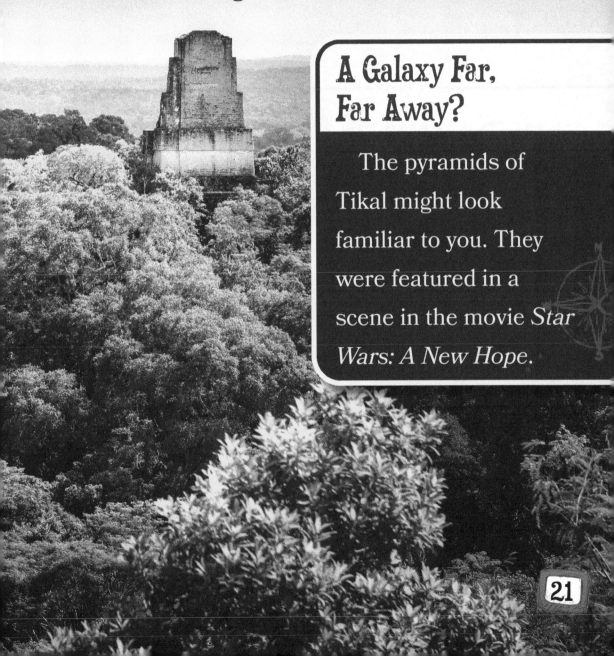

A Galaxy Far, Far Away?

The pyramids of Tikal might look familiar to you. They were featured in a scene in the movie *Star Wars: A New Hope.*

Tikal, Guatemala

Tikal was rediscovered in the mid-19th century. Today you can still see some of the pyramids, palaces, and temples that made Tikal a great city.

Pompeii, Italy

Pompeii was an ancient Roman city home to 10,000 to 20,000 people. In 79 C.E., a volcano named Mount Vesuvius **erupted**. Most Pompeiians saw the eruption and quickly abandoned the city.

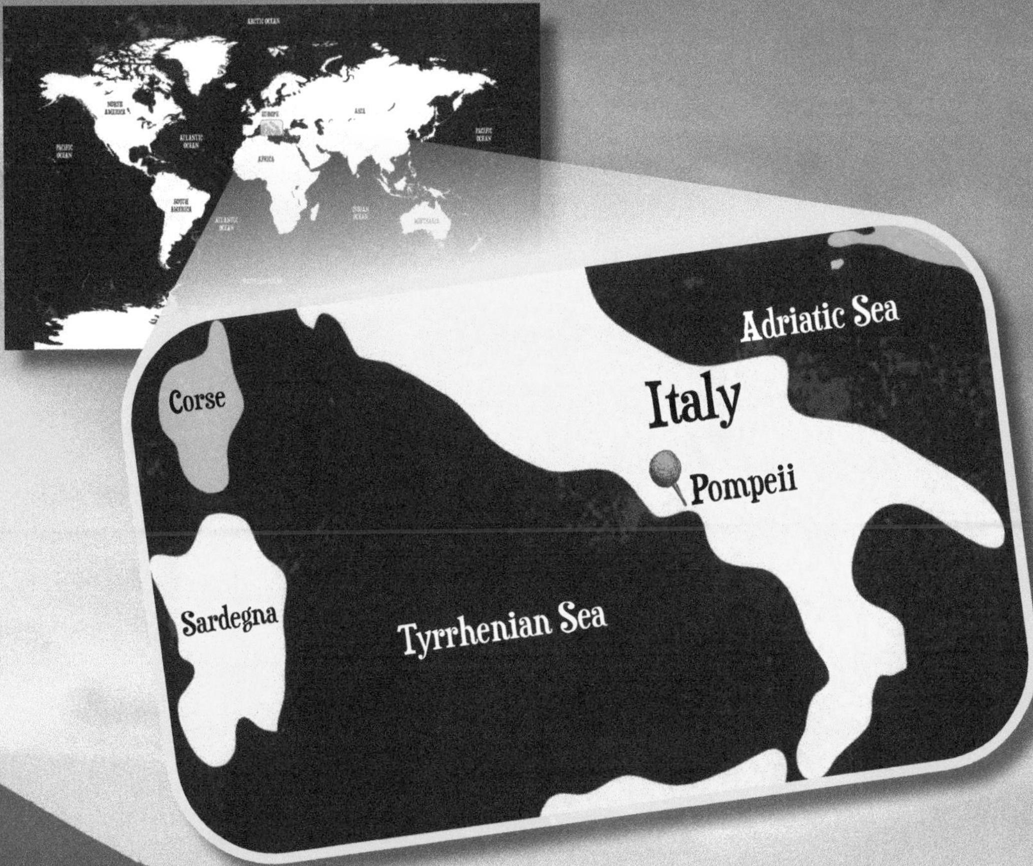
Adriatic Sea
Corse
Italy
Pompeii
Sardegna
Tyrrhenian Sea

erupted (i-RUHPT-id): bursted out lava, hot ashes, and steam

Pompeii, Italy

Volcanic ash rained down on Pompeii after the eruption. Poisonous gas and hot rock flooded the city. Pompeii was buried.

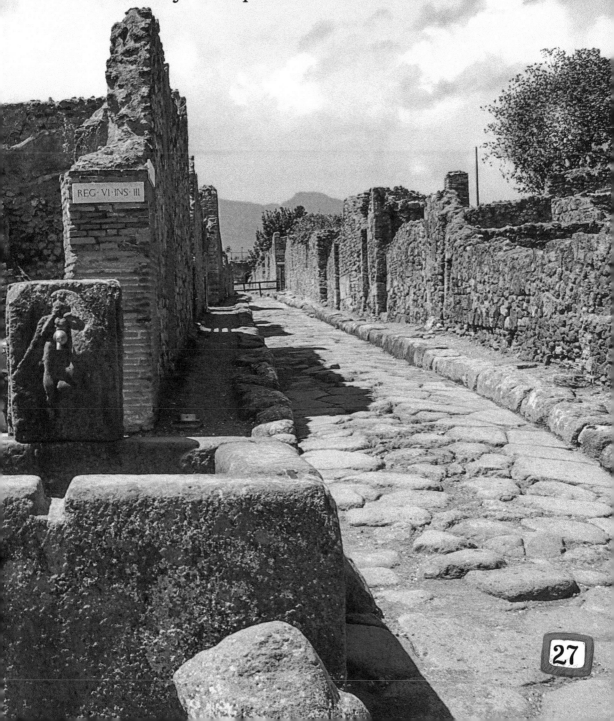

REG·VI·INS·III

Pompeii, Italy

In 1748 explorers rediscovered the city. After digging around Pompeii, they found it looked almos exactly the same as it did when it was buried! Bread was sitting in ovens, skeletons remained buried in the positions in which they died, and whole building were still standing. Pompeii was a city frozen in tim

Memory Game

Look at the pictures. What do you remember reading on the pages where each image appeared?

Index

After-Reading Questions

1. What is a negative effect radiation has had on the wildlife of Chernobyl?

2. What are two safety precautions tourists who visit Chernobyl can take?

3. Why was the town of Bodie founded?

4. What are some buildings you would find in Tikal?

5. Why was Pompeii abandoned?

Activity

Imagine you were going to visit one of the locations from the book. Write a list of questions you would ask a tour guide. See if you can research and find the answers yourself!

About The Author

Hailey Scragg loves learning about and exploring new places. She would like to visit some of these abandoned places someday, especially Tikal. For now she'll keep exploring her city of Columbus, Ohio with her husband and dog.

www.rourkeeducationalmedia.com

PHOTO CREDITS: Cover, page 1: ©francescadani; pages 4-5: ©Ondrej Prosicky; pages 6-7: ©DeSid; page 8, 30: ©EnolaBrain; page 9: ©Roberts Vicups; page 10-11: ©Chistyakosha; page 11a: ©Katsiuba Volha; page 11b, 30: ©Barbara Bednarz; page 12-13, 30: ©PalmsRick; page 14-15: ©CliffBriggin; page 16: ©CREATISTA; page 16-17: ©LifeJourneys; page 18-19, 30: ©Matyas Rehak; page 20-21, 30: ©THPStock; page 22-23: ©James Strachan/robertharding/Newscom; page 24-25, 30: ©mantaphoto; page 26-27: ©nemchinowa; page 28-29: ©Flory; page 29a: ©Xantana; page 29b: ©bruev

Edited by: Madison Capitano
Cover design by: J.J. Giddings
Interior design by: J.J. Giddings

Library of Congress PCN Data

Abandoned Places / Hailey Scragg
(Hidden, Lost, and Discovered)
ISBN 978-1-73164-331-5 (hard cover)
ISBN 978-1-73164-295-0 (soft cover)
ISBN 978-1-73164-363-6 (e-Book)
ISBN 978-1-73164-395-7 (e-Pub)
Library of Congress Control Number: 2020945264

Rourke Educational Media

01-3502011937

CPSIA information can be obtained
at www.ICGtesting.com
Printed in the USA
BVHW021359230522
637143BV00005B/13